MASTER GRANT WRITING

A PROJECT MANAGER'S GUIDE

La Juana Chambers Lawson

MASTER GRANT WRITING

A PROJECT MANAGER'S GUIDE

La Juana Chambers Lawson

Edited by River Walk Publishing, LLC

PUBLISHING, LLC
San Antonio, Texas

Master Grant Writing: A Project Manager's Guide

Publisher: River Walk Publishing LLC

Visit our website at https://growthistacit.com/
Requests for information should be addressed to:
La Juana Chambers Lawson at 210-904-0457 or
growthistacit@gmail.com.

ISBN: 978-1-954787-02-5
e-ISBN/ASIN: 978-1-954787-01-8

Previously published as "A Project Manager's Guide to Grant Writing, Vol. I" electronic version only. This is the first print edition with a new title.

Library of Congress Control Number: 2021902057

Tacit Growth Strategies LLC
2014 S. Hackberry
San Antonio, Texas 78210-3541

Professional Editor & Publisher:
Christopher C. Herring / River Walk Publishing, LLC
www.RiverWalkPublishing.com

Printed and bound in the United States of America

FOREWORD

I am excited for La Juana Chambers Lawson for writing "Master Grant Writing: A Project Manager's Guide". I have been a huge fan of her work and her company Tacit Growth Strategies as a member of the Global Chamber!

I was impressed with her last book which earned Best Selling status and humbled that she included me on the launch of this project as this book's lessons will serve us over many years as a timeless treasure!

Over a 20-year career in the United States Air Force, I enjoyed helping to raise money for nonprofit organizations when Airmen were asked to conduct our annual Combined Federal Campaigns. After I retired and as a chamber of commerce president, vice president of a fundraising division of a major merchant services company and as an executive consultant in fundraising, I know the steps that La Juana has provided us in this book will truly help nonprofits, schools, businesses and faith-based organizations achieve their funding goals.

Raising money is not easy, but "Master Grant Writing: A Project Manager's Guide" makes it easier.

I can recall when I served as a Loaned Executive with the United Way of Bexar County, I met many development directors and grant writers who needed an easy-to-read guide or a reference that could show them the secrets to diversifying their portfolio of revenue streams.

Again, La Juana hit the bull's-eye on meeting this very important need. I look forward to hearing from professionals and students who commit to reading this book as they will find it a gem.

Sadly, during this historic COVID-19 pandemic, the need for money is at the top of the list for organization and business survivability. La Juana's book makes this possible for us to hope and to achieve getting additional funding sources!!!

Congratulations to the author for her fine book!!!

Christopher

Christopher C. Herring
President, River Walk Publishing LLC
Executive Director, Global Chamber San Antonio

Table of Contents

Chapter 1: Introduction   1

Chapter 2: Parts of the Whole   15

Chapter 3: First, Project Management   23

Chapter 4: Second, Staging the entity or readying the
organization   33

Chapter 5: Third, Digital Inclusion   45

Chapter 6: Fourth, Collaboration   55

Chapter 7: Fifth, Governance   61

Chapter 8: Conclusion   69

REFERENCES   71

ABOUT THE AUTHOR   73

List of Figures

Figure 1 Hedging Bets for Grant Success   5

Figure 2 Some Grant Writing Assumptions & Constraints   8

Figure 3 Grant Writing in Sum   13

Figure 4 What is Grant Writing?   17

Figure 5 Grant Writing Components   17

Figure 6 Grant Writing Group vs Team   20

DEDICATION

This book is dedicated to Tacit Growers all over the world.

Opportunities to grow are all around us.

Remember to breathe,

Reset your mind for abundance rather than scarcity, and

Be open to try new things when you are most vulnerable.

Learning is perpetual.

A soaked sponge is set.

A dry sponge is mobile.

I hope that this book carries you to and through success in thought and practice.

Chapter 1

Introduction

Porsha was dismayed.

After fifteen hours of nonstop toil (and what she felt was *over* preparation), Porsha learned that the nonprofit she had volunteered to write a grant for wasn't actually eligible for a grant after all. She found out within seconds of submitting the grant and all of its attachments, which resulted in a 45MB file of all sorts of information ranging from the application itself to monthly records of payroll withholdings to prove that the organization had staff and was a reputable employer for more than one year.

"Entity ineligible: please read grant instructions to all applicants".

She immediately thought to herself, "How could this happen?" Porsha had completed the grant application checklist from the grantor's website.

She even had a previously submitted grant from another entity that was successfully awarded for guidance and quick reference.

So, how could the entity be immediately rejected?

When Porsha learned of the ineligibility, she phoned Tracy, the organization's Executive Director (ED), to share the unfortunate news. The ED didn't initially receive the news well. She was certain that the rejection was a technical error of some sort. Tracy then remembered a correspondence from that grantor sent to her official email address relating to a previous grant submission. She was one of two of the organization's grant officials copied on the email. She shared with Porsha that the email was unread, then forwarded it to her. Porsha read the email and subsequently found out that the entity had recently applied for the same grant during a different funding cycle and was denied then because their work did not match the grantor's funding priorities. Unbeknownst to Porsha and Tracy (*because she didn't read the email*), the grantor shared a detailed rejection letter as an attachment to an email in response to the previous grant writer for the organization who resigned from her role at the entity a month before Porsha arrived to help with grants.

Interestingly, Tracy was genuinely surprised to learn that the organization was denied a second time for funding as she had been cultivating a relationship with one of the grantor's executives in its c-suite. She thought that the grant pursuit was sure to be looked upon favorably. That's why she sought Porsha's expertise and support.

What Porsha should have done upon hire is to conduct a needs assessment for the organization. Taking circumspect account of the organization's needs would have helped her determine what grant opportunities are best suited for the organization. Porsha was wrong for preparing a grant application for the organization without having the information that Tracy later revealed to her. A simple consultation with Tracy during the process of conducting a needs assessment would have helped Porsha discover which entities the organization had applied previously, which funders rejected their applications or requests for funding, and why those applications and requests were denied.

Ultimately, both Porsha and Tracy learned two key lessons. And that is to never take relationships for granted. Decisions aren't made in vacuums or by solitary agents. And, probably most importantly, grants aren't free money.

Grant writing is one of the most popular means of securing financial investment in support of an individual or organization's expenses incurred to produce a particular product, service, or result. Generally, grants are pursued by individuals and/or organizations to supplement, not supplant *(we'll talk more about this in Chapter 2)*, revenue streams supporting existing general operations and/or project budgets. There are a plethora of assumptions and constraints involved in the pursuit of grants that can devolve an individual's or organization's good intentions into rather ruinous consequences when not handled with care.

This book endeavors to disentangle grant writing with real-life examples of what to do (*as well as what not to do*) as it relates to pursuing and writing grants.

Now you may be wondering, so what then is grant writing?

Grant writing, in all of its mystery and growing sophistication, is a misnomer. That's right. Grant writing is a misnomer; it's a totally inaccurate and incomplete though really common reference to an entire profession that can only be understood as the sum of several parts.

What is grant writing?

I like to think of grant writing as the most creative, integrative, and rigorous tool in an individual or organization's fundraising toolkit. Grant writing is one part of a fundraising plan that should be analyzed for expected (*or planned*) benefits or rewards and their associated costs or risks (*or actuals*).

 ***Pro Tip:***

One way to determine whether grant writing is a worthy pursuit for you and/or your business (i.e., for-profit or nonprofit) is to conduct a cost-benefit analysis. This is an important first (analytical) step towards building confidence in making a decision. Every decision you make is a bet. Just like bets, decisions come with associated risks that are simply accepted, mitigated, or rejected. And just like bets, we risk more when we're confident in our chances of winning or gaining something in return.

As a decision-maker, identifying and properly assessing risks associated with making certain decisions, like pursuing grants, for example, is of paramount importance. Inflows and outflows, like costs or risks and benefits or rewards, should be top of mind so taking risks, or simply making a decision, is principled and objective.

Making decisions, especially tough ones, sometimes feels like an all-or-nothing matter. When we make decisions, we may go all-in but most of the time, we go *some-in* to protect ourselves against losing everything. In the real world, effective decision-makers actively hedge their bets to increase the likelihood of favorable returns. In pursuing grants, this may look like:

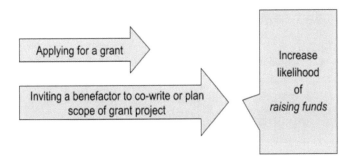

Figure 1   Hedging Bets for Grant Success

Identifying and properly assessing risks associated with making decisions inherently supports that it is necessary to take risks to turn a profit, or make an improvement, or take a chance on an opportunity.

Example:

You research a grant opportunity with an announced award ceiling of $300,000 and award floor of $100,000. This means that, if your grant project is selected for award, it has the likelihood to be awarded anywhere between $100,000 to $300,000. The reward is pretty clear. Presented as a range between award floor and ceiling, you hope to achieve the

$300,000 award. Though, to realistically compete for a grant award in that amount, you must invest a considerable amount of money. The amount you must invest is the sum of the time and resources, plus any eligible opportunity costs associated with choosing this particular grant opportunity over others, necessary to achieve a grant application that could be considered competitive and eligible for award.

I would like to share a story to help convey the investment that is (really) required when pursuing a grant opportunity or not.

No matter the amount being requested, writing a grant is an extremely rigorous one that impacts and involves every aspect of leading and operating a business. Here's a lesson learned from one client whose real identity has been concealed for anonymity and privacy purposes:

Why don't we have a grant yet?

Meena is the President and Board Chair of a newly established nonprofit 501(c)(3) charitable organization. The charity has no staff and is run entirely by volunteers. Members of Meena's small but mighty Board of Directors have high hopes for the organization. They have extraordinarily bullish sentiment about the prospect of the charity receiving a large grant. So Meena places a discussion on the agenda under new business for the Board's next meeting. She's genuinely curious to better understand the Board's optimism about the organization applying for and receiving a grant given their newness and lack of operating infrastructure and support. To Meena, applying for a grant requires a great deal of preparation on her part.

As President of the charity, she will have to decide operating procedures, develop operating and project budgets, assemble and manage a team, and even institute governance to ensure good record-keeping and tracking in accordance with evidence-based best practices and statutory requirements.

As Chair of the Board of Directors, Meena will have to lead the development of the charity's organizational documents, i.e., its General Bylaws, Constitution (if eligible), and financials, develop standards for everything from Board expectations to committee assignments, and train the Board in the many tactics associated with making an organization grant eligible. Another duty of Meena will be to develop a schedule and script for members of the Board to meet, whether in-person and/or virtually, with key decision-makers and influencers in the grant-making and philanthropic community.

So, the big day arrives and Meena calls the meeting to order. Attendance is taken and meeting minutes from the previous meeting are briefly discussed to set the tone for the new business that Meena is anxiously awaiting to get to. The minutes are approved, old business is finished and Meena has timed and set the agenda to have just one item for discussion (and possible action) under new business. Before she shares her thoughts, Meena poses a question to the board for moderated discussion to probe into their bullish sentiment about pursuing grants for the charity.

"As you all know, we are a newly established charity with no doubt a great future ahead but lots of work to do in order to realize that future as a working board. I appreciate your fervor and interest in wanting to grow our charitable work and impact with support from our philanthropic community. Why do you think we should pursue a grant at this point in time?" Ana is the Board Secretary; she keeps attendance, takes minutes and records the business of the Board meetings, so Meena called for her to help moderate the discussion.

"Well, I personally believe that this organization must get a grant in order to grow", said one board member. "I learn of grants that I think that we are perfect for all of the time. I think that *not* pursuing grants is leaving tons of money on the table", said another board member.

Let's quickly note the many assumptions and constraints at play with Meena's Board.

ID	Description	Validation	Status
Assumption #1	To grow, the organization needs a grant.	Belief, generally held with little to no empirical data or proof	Not Valid
Assumption #2	Not pursuing grants leaves a lot of money on the table.	This is just FOMO talking *FOMO = Fear of missing out	Not Valid
Assumption #3	Our organization is grant eligible.	Same as above #1	Not Valid
Constraint #1	Newly established charity with little to no records, reputation for being well managed and led, or standard operations.	---	---

Constraint #2	Working board of members who may or may not have the capacity to organize a start-up to scale without experienced and reliable staff.	---	---
Constraint #3	Being newly established means that the organization will have very limited spending records and transactions; ergo, the organization will not have valid operating or project budgets.	---	---

Figure 2   Some Grant Writing Assumptions & Constraints

Taking quick inventory of assumptions and constraints is a critical component of getting clear on the associated benefits and costs should you decide to do something, especially as a Board carrying equal fiduciary responsibility to properly managing a charity.

So, for this example, Meena should conduct a simplified reward to risk calculation with her Board to help them make a confident and more objective decision on how to move the discussion forward or to collectively decide not to move the discussion forward.

A simplified reward to risk calculation should be done it two parts:

Part One: Gaining Clarity

Question #1: What is your risk appetite?

Question #2: What is your risk tolerance level? This should

be asked in general and for different types of risks that you think will be common in your line of work.

Question #3: What risk(s) are you willing to accept if things don't go as planned? This ties back into your risk appetite but leads quite naturally into your ideal reward to risk ratio that should function as something of a standard or bar you set to govern how you arrive at a decision.

Part Two: Setting the bar

If I make this decision, then I am expecting to get ____ in return for risking ____.

Meena's Board of Directors are overwhelmingly risk-averse. When Meena utters the word *risk* to members of the Board, they hold their breaths in fright and nervousness. Meena is quite risk-tolerant as a leader, however. Her risk tolerance propels the organization forward and this goes largely unknown and unappreciated by her Board. They have a profound tendency to want something for nothing. For an organization like theirs, wanting something for nothing is not uncommon. Though the harm that is committed to professionals, especially those who may be less socioeconomically mobile, minorities, or LGBTQIA+, cannot be overstated when communities are supported by nonprofits who will not employ or financially compensate for the value that experts and professionals bring to scale and sustain the work and purpose of an organization. This sort of organizational culture is unempowering and antithetical to collaboration, inclusion, and high performance. As President and Board Chair, Meena has to decide and shape the culture of the nonprofit she leads and manages. From an operational standpoint, getting something for nothing on the Board and among volunteers is largely unsustainable (and unrealistic) for the nonprofit. After all, the startup needs to establish organizational and project budgets by actually realizing its expenses. And best practices for the startup must be accountable and calculable to be reproduced for desired results and to sustain the organization. So Meena called a special Board meeting to discuss the organization's risk appetite, holding that every official act or decision of the Board would involve an upfront investment and an associated risk to exploit in favorable situations or mitigate in unfavorable situations. "For every dollar that we invest into the pursuit of a new endeavor, like pursuing grant opportunities, for example, what is the minimum that we expect to get in return?" Because my risk appetite is tenacious, I actively seek suitable opportunities for my business that require a solid investment upfront for the chance to do business that is four times or double the value of what I initially invested. Should the opportunity present itself, I will spend days preparing competitive proposals that may result in my business being awarded a contract that is worth at least double my firm's existing contracts, ideally four times as much.

Business leaders conduct cost-benefit analyses to decide the efficacy and salience of certain policies and procedures in relation to projects that support their organization's work and purpose. Depending on the opportunity at hand, a cost-benefit analysis may be more appropriate as an exercise for the Board and/or leadership of the organization.

So, what's your takeaway?

Grant writing is a serious fundraising tactic that to be fruitful and prove worthwhile, must be an organizational commitment. Total system buy-in predisposes grant projects for success. And even more importantly, total system buy-in for grant writing pursuits serves as a solid foundation to high performance for the organization in the near, mid, and long terms. The experience of pursuing grants as a cohesive team is a great morale booster for an already well managed and led entity looking to scale with partner entities and the philanthropic community.

Chapter 2

Parts of the Whole

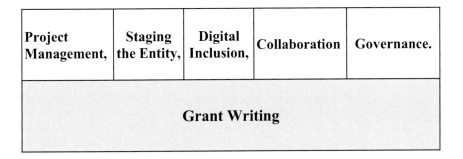

Project Management,	Staging the Entity,	Digital Inclusion,	Collaboration	Governance.
Grant Writing				

Figure 3   Grant Writing in Sum

My experience with writing grants and proposals has spanned more than a decade. And what a wild ride it's been!

I have seen the ruin of a thirty years old nonprofit organization brought on by the award of a multi-million-dollar grant because of their lack of leadership. And I've seen the growth, scale, and sophistication of a nonprofit organization that wasn't even a year old brought on by the award of a multi-million-dollar grant that advanced their business model and guiding principles.

After all of these years, the greatest lesson I have learned is that grant writing involves so much and none of it can be skipped or fast-forwarded if you want to put your best foot forward. One of my most memorable experiences was writing grants and proposals for an international organization at the tender age of 18 years old. Interestingly, the organization did not view their work and purpose as a solution to a problem, though the case could be made that their work did solve a problem (or two) in the international community they served. Rather, they viewed their work and purpose as a necessary addition and contribution to the global community. I was so enamored with the organization I volunteered to do all of the following and a whole lot more:

- find suitable grant opportunities for them,
- write grant applications and proposals,
- introduce the founders to key decision-makers from the philanthropic community who could support the organization financially,
- recruit and train volunteers and groom organizational leaders (to include prospective Board members), and
- ready the organization to formally receive support from the philanthropic community with official financial records and statements, telecommunications, facilities, staff members, and digital infrastructure to keep everyone on task, in-the-know, and plugged into the impact of the organization with just a couple of clicks.

I took great pride in the work I did. And I believe that my sense of pride and consistent can-do-attitude attracted other talent and philanthropists to support the organization in the short, medium and long terms. Politics plays a huge role in grant writing and, more generally, pursuing grants. Outside of being who gets what, when, where, how, and for how long, politics in the context of grants is about who's visible or has the attention of the masses and for how many generations. For this and several other reasons, having good leadership matters. In simple terms, good leadership will attract good attention. Bad leadership will bring chaos and drama, and is the hallmark of ineffective organizations. The organizations who are most visible get to stay visible due to their ability to emotionally connect to a wide audience. Think about some of your favorite charities to support. Do you believe in their leadership? Would you give to the organization on a monthly, quarterly, or annual basis if you didn't believe in the organization's leadership? Well, maybe you aren't familiar with the leadership of the organization because your allegiance and pledge may not be to any particular leader. Your allegiance and pledge to donate may be to the organization at large because you believe in its programming or mission or all of the above. Though if you give to the same charities on a consistent basis like I do, then I'm sure that you have faith in the charity's leadership to do what's right and to spend those dollars that you and many others donate ethically. Organizations with good leadership secure your donations with frequent solicitations, handwritten thank you letters signed by the Board and staff, personalized emails providing you opportunities to see your donation at work (sometimes even in real-time).

I've observed time and time again that organizations that take proper inventory of their strengths, weaknesses, opportunities, and threats, and find ways to leverage and exploit their strengths, get visible and stay visible. Results-oriented and visionary leadership is the most valuable strength an organization can have.

I did for that international organization what many

volunteers have done for nonprofit and even for-profit entities. I wasn't interested in being paid. I simply wanted to prove to myself that I could do what I love to do well enough to make it a career rather than just a hobby. To be honest, I was so new to the professional grant writing world that I wouldn't know where to start to figure out how much I should be paid, at what frequency, and what to invoice as billable work versus in-kind to the organization.

Before I resigned and moved on to fully commit to my academic pursuits, I recorded that my work at that international organization resulted in them being successfully awarded $4.2 Million USD in grant contracts and direct contributions. It was an honor then and remains an honor now to know that my work had such a major impact on the sustainability of the organization. Over the years, I have noticed that they have leveraged those early contributions for more and others throughout the global philanthropic community. From what I have gathered from friends in philanthropic circles, the organization now grosses tens of millions each year in support of their noble mission, purpose, and work throughout the global community. Their success brings me great honor and pride.

There are many approaches to successful grant writing. There is no one-size-fits-all in successful grant writing. Though I find that most of my success in grant writing as a seasoned professional involves the mastery of these parts of the whole:

- Project management,
- Staging the entity or readying the organization,
- Digital inclusion,
- Collaboration, and
- Governance.

This spider chart is a graphical representation of the most important components of grant writing that, with varying degrees of involvement, can make or break the success of your grant project:

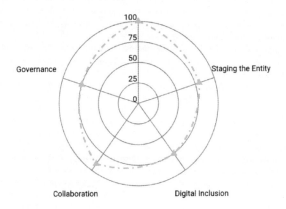

Figure 4   What is Grant Writing?

In this figure, the five components are graphically displayed on a radar or spider chart to show their commonality in relation to their degree of intensity or involvement.

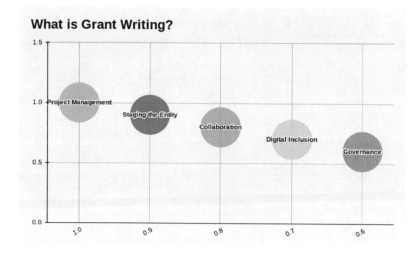

Figure 5   Grant Writing Components

In this figure, the five components of grant writing are plotted in relation to their degree of intensity or involvement. The varying degrees of intensity or involvement are based upon experience, observation and a survey of lessons learned documentation from awarded grant projects across multiple sectors spanning ten calendar years beginning in the year 2010. Note this plot shows a comprehensive approach to writing grants that is considered both emotionally intelligent and rigorous in practice. Each component is independently evaluated on a scale of 1 or 100% in measure of the degree of intensity or involvement over the lifecycle of a given grant writing pursuit.

These are the five parts of the whole commonly known, but grossly misunderstood.

Let's take time to discuss each component of grant writing.

Chapter 3

First, Project Management

P roject Management can be defined as the art of coordinating resources and directing cross-functional teams so the components of work performed by each team produce frequent value to the customer(s) with a stake in the project.

Projects are chartered to create value.

The Project Management Institute defines a project as a "temporary endeavor undertaken to produce a unique product, service, or result". It's important to remember that grants are projects and should be managed as such.

Grant projects are comprehensive and integrative. They should have a clear focus and be organized by coordinated tactics to produce consistent value through individual components of work on results-oriented teams.

Grant writing is an endeavor that should involve a cross-functional team of:

1. Planned beneficiaries,
2. Grant project champions,

3. Experts,
4. Innovators,
5. Visionaries, and in *some* more experienced/structured circumstances
6. Benefactors.

Each grant writing pursuit should be led by a Project Manager who is responsible for leading and managing teams to solve scoped problems with near, mid and long-term Agile SMART-oriented solutions.

Grant writing teams are groups who work interdependently together to complete a task. Grant writing teams share leadership among team members and decide work assignments by delegation rather than simple assignment.

Group	**Team**
A collection of individuals who work *independently* together to complete a task	A group with *shared* aim and goals who work *interdependently* to complete a task
Strong, independent leader who functions like a manager	Shared leadership and vision between members
Plan, Do, Check, Act	Plan, Do, Check, Learn, Act
Accomplish individual goals	Accomplish team goals
No teamwork, work alone	Teamwork, work together

Figure 6   Grant Writing Group vs Team

Grant-writing teams, rather than grant-writing groups, are uniquely qualified to produce competitive grant project plans and proposals.

The lifecycle of grant projects is quite agile and iterative rather than linear, serial, and sequential. Due to the fluid nature of grant project planning, adjustments are commonly made throughout the grant project lifecycle. Adjustments are usually made to create value throughout the process rather than simply at the end or close of the project. This is a fundamental feature of agile project management.

Grant projects are agile through and through. The inevitability of change is accommodated as the grant project is broken into its smallest parts or components of work and prioritized by teams who drive to deliver maximum value often.

Value is created consistently and is used to elicit feedback that will improve the customer experience throughout the grant project's lifecycle. This also ensures a smooth transition when closing the project but not disbanding the team. Let's be honest. Ordinary grant project lifecycles usually end but not the team that made it all happen. Grant awards and grant projects are leveraged for opportunities made successful due to the unique expertise and perspectives of cross-functional teams assembled by the organization in support of grant project pursuits and awards. In an unpredictable world, the true value of agile grant projects is in its empowerment of the team over the process.

During his keynote at an Open Space Network Event hosted by the Computer History Museum, political advisor and best-selling author Jeremy Rifkin said that "by 2030, we're likely to have ubiquitous interconnectivity. We're creating a planetary brain and nervous center with zero marginal costs".

In a knowledge and project-based economy, how individuals and organizations communicate value so it may be perceived by their benefactors or customers is overwhelmingly technological. Value must be data-oriented and communicated rapidly (and through different mediums and platforms in line with the preferences of your benefactors or customers). And then there's the critical realization that to ensure that your organization is spending most of its time performing value-add activities, your organization's data/information architecture has to mirror that of your customers and/or benefactors. We'll discuss this more in Digital Inclusion.

Grants and proposals are information technology-dependent. The process of pursuing grants, preparing for a particular grant opportunity, submitting the grant, and hopefully receiving and retaining the grant is information technology-dependent. As systems are becoming more and more sophisticated and interconnected, those who are interested in applying for grants or otherwise formally procuring business with other for-profit and/or nonprofit businesses must become technologically savvy or hire someone who is.

Corporations and public entities are held accountable for their charitable giving and philanthropy. Charitable giving and philanthropy are not fixed. They are variable due to changes in tax laws (*see the Internal Revenue Code*), the financial state of corporations and other contributing factors associated with the global marketplace.

Project management and agile are modus operandi for grantees and grant seekers. Responding to change as an accountable and empowered team is the only reasonable way to respond to change. Agile project management features teams who manage change by taking collective responsibility for the big-picture goals of the project, use appropriate agile methodologies or hybrids to gather, deliver, and track requests from the customer, and leverage knowledge that can be optimized against the law of diminishing returns as lessons learned and best practices.

A successful traditional project has these characteristics:

- The project is *within scope,* meaning only the work planned and approved to be done is what's actually being performed.

- The project is *on or ahead of schedule,* meaning that value is being delivered on time (*or as planned*) or earlier than expected per the term or contract period.

- The project is *on or behind budget or costs,* meaning that the expenses associated with performing the work for the project is going as planned (or on par) or is less than expected.

A successful agile project has these characteristics:

- The project leverages ambiguity to create value specific to the sponsor's requests, meaning that the project's scope of work is variable rather than fixed, allowing the team to break up the project into several stages with frequent collaboration with sponsors and continuous improvement at each stage.

- The project is *on or ahead of schedule,* meaning that

value is being delivered on time (*or as planned*) or earlier than expected per the term or contract period.

☐ The project is *on or behind budget or costs*, meaning that the expenses associated with performing the work for the project is going as planned (or on par) or is less than expected.

The four key values and relative meaning of <u>agile</u> are:

☐ Individuals and interactions over processes and tools, meaning that an accountable and empowered grant project team are more critical to the mission than processes, protocols, and tools. Think of your grant project team. The team performs best when (1) the team knows one another and understands each other's strengths, (2) the team is organized within the context of an experimental culture where they are encouraged to move from what it is towards what's possible, and (3) communication between members of the team is frequent, open, and trustworthy. Valuing the team over processes and tools respects the reality that processes and tools will change while your team will collaboratively evolve together to deliver an optimized grant project.

☐ Working software over comprehensive documentation, meaning that the agile grant project team's focus is on delivering value to its customer rather than documentation. This is how the team can create value for your customer and deliver it rapidly. For organizations interested in pursuing grants or retaining and leveraging awarded grants, this means that the agile grant team is primarily customer-focused and mission-oriented. Therefore, the organization must ensure that documentation and record-keeping are the responsibility of a more traditional project management team for grant purposes as grants are data-intensive and customers will need to have data beyond the scope of any given project and is more organization or systems-wide.

- ☐ Customer collaboration over contract negotiation, meaning that the agile grant project team is customer-facing and customer first. Customer first teams are organized to meet customer needs, create positive experiences that help to strengthen the brand and reputation of the organization, and bring satisfaction to your customers. This means that procurement issues and other legal or contractual matters should not be handled or known by the agile grant project team. Contract negotiations are usually handled by Project Managers. For the agile grant project team, the functional manager relegated to handling procurement matters for the organization should be the sole responsible party for any contract negotiations or similar matters.

- ☐ Responding to change over following a plan, meaning that the agile grant project team is assembled to lead and manage change. The agile grant project team decides how to respond to change by using a variety of applicable methodologies and combinations. This means that the team drives improvements and innovation on the project by taking the initiative to do so rather than having a traditionally heavy reliance upon project architecture, i.e., planning, processes, or tactical execution.

Grant projects are chartered to create value and to strengthen society's safety net. Most organizations aspire to be an agile organization. Though this aspiration must begin with a very fundamental understanding of traditional project management. In practice, traditional project management epitomizes planning the work and working the plan. Helped by global evidence-based best practices and lessons learned, an organization-wide commitment to traditional project management is a business playbook that is worth its weight in gold.

Combined, traditional project management and agile are future-proof approaches to leading, managing, and fundamentally operating a business anywhere in the world.

Chapter 4

Second, Staging the entity or readying the organization

S taging the entity or readying the organization interested in pursuing a grant entails all of the steps necessary to ensure that an entity is grant eligible. Generally, these steps are sorted and taken care of prior to the creation of social media and websites for the organization. For charitable nonprofits, a founding Board of Directors should be in place and overseeing each of the steps.

Grant eligibility or preparedness involves some of the following:

- ▢ Establishing a legal status for the entity,

- ▢ Instituting leadership (volunteer and paid) that will inspire faith and trust in the corporate and philanthropic communities you will seek support from,

- ▢ Clarifying your mission, vision, goals, and objectives,

- ▢ Engaging in strategic planning at a frequency that accommodates the organization's (most) major milestones,

- ▢ Determining an internal financial and program audit schedule, protocols, and Board oversight committee,

- Determining an external financial and program audit schedule, protocols, and Board governance,

- Having clearly defined program goals and frequently measured performance indicators,

- Ensuring a strong web presence highlighting what you do well (in as comprehensive a manner as possible) and often,

- Solidifying a competitive and comprehensive technology plan,

- Hiring subject matter experts, whether on staff or contracted as professional and contracted services, to predispose your organization for success regarding information architecture and a competitive advantage,

- Ensure that all of the organization's invoices align with project and program budgets as well as organizational strategic priorities,

- Having an active SAM registration and DUNS number,

- Having an Employer Identification Number (EIN),

- Having at least three years of tax filings to the state and nation,

- Having at least three years of Board approved financial statements,

- Having at least $40,000 in budget expenses in the most recent fiscal year,

- Evidence of payroll withholding for at least one paid staff member.

All of the above are critical success factors for readying an organization for a grant pursuit. Rushing into grant pursuits *can* result in favorable outcomes. However, more often than not, rushing into grant pursuits will result in outcomes that can be constructively regarded as first-hand lessons learned.

Sometimes, rushing into grant pursuits can hurt your brand, growth potential and reputation. Let's dive into evidence-based best practices for each of the critical success factors to prevent you from bringing irreparable harm to your brand, growth potential, or reputation.

Establishing a legal status for the entity.

There are loads of grant opportunities for individuals and organizations. Generally, individuals seeking to submit a grant application for a funding opportunity (i.e., as an individual unattached to a particular agency or entity) may only apply to opportunities open to individuals. Usually, individuals are required to register an account on a grant portal or other grant management software platform in order to evidence their legal existence, expertise, references, and residence. Organizations interested in pursuing grants must have proof of their legal status. This documentation is usually conferred by the state that the organization is formed or registered to do business in. If the organization is a tax-exempt organization, they should be formally recognized by the IRS on this site. Individual-specific and organizational grant opportunities are regularly posted on grants.gov and philanthropynewsdigest.org.

Instituting leadership (volunteer and paid) that will inspire faith and trust in the corporate and philanthropic communities you will seek support from.

Community leaders and subject experts are to organizations what Patrick Mahomes II is to the Kansas City Chiefs. With them, your organization is limitless. You can attract and recruit incredible talent, place them into volunteer and paid roles for the organization according to clear expectations, scoped job descriptions with deliverable schedules, professionally develop them through mentorship and networking, and retain them through passion and professionalism. Corporate and philanthropic communities are always looking to join established teams of movers and shakers with conspicuous potential. Supporting established teams of movers and shakers with palpable and visible potential inspire passion, trust, and sustainable support for organizations seeking stability and the ability to pivot when opportunities arise.

Clarifying your mission, vision, goals, and objectives.

Well worded and well demonstrated mission, vision, goal, and objective statements are critical to organizational efficacy. Felix Dennis once said that "having a great idea is simply not enough. It is how ideas are implemented that counts in the long run."[1]

---

[1] Dennis, Felix (2011). The Narrow Road: A Brief Guide to the Getting of Money, ISBN: 9781101476420.

Engaging in strategic planning at a frequency that accommodates the organization's (most) major milestones.

According to the IRS, a tax year is an annual accounting period for keeping records and reporting income and expenses or revenues. Unless otherwise required, organizations adopt or determine their own tax year or accounting period based upon several factors to include their frequency or schedule of bookkeeping or record keeping, their time in existence throughout the year, and their entity or filing status. Plenty of organizations have fiscal years that start on January 1 and end on the last day of the last month of the year (December 31). And plenty of organizations have fiscal years that start on October 1 and end on September 30 - this is largely due to the lifecycle of their grant awards.

Determining an internal financial and program audit schedule, protocols, and Board oversight committee.

The Board of Directors, if the organization has one, are charged with regularly reviewing financial statements during every Board meeting. They are also charged with financial oversight to ensure that the organization is meeting internal financial and program protocols, statutory regulations and any other obligations. Generally, a Finance Committee is established with Board members who elect to serve, subject experts (e.g., a CPA on the Board or a community leader who is financially literate may volunteer to serve on the committee), and a short list of the organization's staff. Usually, the Board develops and monitors budgets, manages cash, creates financial policies and procedures, monitors the organization's spending and allocation of resources. Altogether, members of the Finance Committee are organized to operationalize the day-to-day financial monitoring and oversight of the organization.

Determining an external financial and program audit schedule, protocols, and Board governance.

The Board of Directors, if the organization has one, are charged with regularly reviewing financial statements during every Board meeting. They are also charged with financial oversight to ensure that the organization is meeting external financial and program protocols, statutory regulations and any other obligations like GAAP for nonprofits. Generally, a Finance Committee is established with Board members who are recruited to serve, subject experts (e.g., a CPA on the Board or a community leader who is financially literate may volunteer to serve on the committee), and a short list of the organization's staff. Usually, the Board develops and monitors budgets, manages cash, creates financial policies and procedures, monitors the organization's spending and allocation of resources. Altogether, members of the Finance Committee are organized to prepare an organization for an independent audit of the organization's finances and programs.

Having clearly defined program goals and frequently measured performance indicators.

Designing a program involves planning, doing, checking, acting, learning with a team of cross-functional subject experts, and starting the cycle all over again (and possibly again). For this reason and others, program design is quite iterative. Goal-setting, like program design, is critical to predisposing a program for success. Through setting (agile) SMART goals for a program, the team can better accomplish an intended service, product, or result one documented and achieved milestone at a time.

Ensuring a strong web presence highlighting what you do well (in as comprehensive a manner as possible) and often.

Your website is the most important marketing tool you have. Traditional and paid advertising, Search Engine Optimization (SEO), Google Adwords, email campaigns, social media marketing, etc. all lead back to your website. Accessibility and language are key to ensuring a usable website that helps visitors learn more about your organization, sign-up to stay in touch with your organization, and even decide to financially support one of your programs. Being mindful of and actively reducing the Digital Divide is your responsibility as well; this will be discussed in the next chapter.

Solidifying a competitive and comprehensive technology plan.

Technology planning is necessary to determine program-level and organization-specific information architecture, to include its planned inventory of devices, wired and wireless connectivity, software, hardware, technology budget(s), and learning/training schedules.

Hiring subject experts, whether on staff or contracted, for a competitive advantage.

Hiring subject experts to complete components of work for a program or for the organization overall builds budgets, clarifies tactical expectations for organizational leadership, and brings visibility to your organization. Hiring subject experts, rather than relying upon unpaid labor or time and effort, is critical to ensuring that the organization has reliable and valid budget expenses and (hopefully) associated revenue streams.

Ensure that the organization's accounts payable and receivable align with program and organizational budgets as well as short, medium, and long-term strategic priorities.

As a follow-up to ensuring clear program goals, the organization's short-term and recurring debts should be acknowledged and referred to in reasonable detail within the organization's strategic plan. The same goes for the organization's unrestricted and restricted assets. Both of which should be subject to Board (if eligible) oversight in observation of and compliance with evidence-based best practices and lessons learned.

Having an active SAM registration and DUNS number.

Often, grant makers and funders within the corporate, government, and philanthropic communities require individuals and organizations to have an active System of Award Management (SAM) and Dun & Bradstreet Data Universal Number System (DUNS) number.

Having an Employer Identification Number (EIN).

Sometimes, grant makers and funders within the corporate, government, and philanthropic communities require only an EIN to apply for grants and to be awarded a grant contract.

Having at least three years of tax filings.

Organizations with more time in service have more potential of being successfully awarded grants due to the learning curve effect. Entities with annual independent finance and program audits fare better than those without.

Having at least $40,000 in budget expenses in the most recent fiscal year.

Tsh Oxenreider once said that "the simplest definition of budgeting is telling your money where to go".[2] A general rule of thumb for organizations pursuing grants is to remember to be mindful of your ask. Grant makers and funders are not likely to give an organization with a micro or small budget more than they have actually raised or spent.

Evidence of payroll withholding for at least one paid staff member.

Sometimes, grant makers and funders within the corporate, government, and philanthropic communities require grant seekers have at least one paid staff member. If and when you hire staff, take great records for prospective grantors.

As a grant writing professional and grant reviewer, I have lost count of how often I've encountered organizations that pursued grants without having just a handful of the aforementioned critical success factors. Though shooting your shot is better than sitting on your hands and letting opportunities go by, organizations need to take the pursuit of

---

[2] Oxenreider, Tsh (2010). Organized Simplicity: The Clutter-Free Approach to Intentional Living, ASIN: B004AM5IJW.

grant opportunities as seriously as they take transacting business with public and/or private entities. Grant awards are contracts. They are legal documents and can dramatically affect an organization not found within compliance or not satisfactorily completing the components of work stipulated in the awarded contract.

Chapter 5

✑

Third, Digital Inclusion

How does Digital Inclusion, or the lack thereof, impact grant writing pursuits? I learned about the Digital Divide while working as a grant writer for a school district. Here's what happened.

I was hired by a historically underfunded school district as a grant professional with a proven record of writing and managing grants from inception through to closure. One of my main motivations for wanting to work for the district was really my passion as a STEM educator for making access to learning cool, fun, and inclusive. Additionally, I was motivated to bring some good to a historically underserved and underrepresented school district with students who weren't afforded the same opportunities that other students were simply because of their zip codes.

For nearly two decades, the school district had been unable to secure grants to support some of the exceptional needs of its twenty campuses that couldn't be adequately addressed by general funds. I dedicated over fifty hours during my first week of working for the district gathering as much information as I could. The need was so profound all over the district - in the schools and in the homes of the students. I remember carrying my laptop with me to each campus. I would informally question most all of the campus staff beginning with the clerks or receptionists, custodians, and kitchen staff. After meeting with the campus teachers, counselors, and principals, I inventoried the needs of the campuses. I would go back to my office to analyze and organize the inventory of needs for each school campus by category or type, its impact (i.e. how many students were impacted by the need), and its scope of influence (i.e. if addressing that need would alleviate needs elsewhere and for how long). After ranking the needs, I would decide a course of action that would jumpstart my grant management lifecycle with an intent to begin planning with an appropriate, cross-functional grant project team.

The most common need across the school district was technology. The district did not have a reliable cable or wireless network. Teachers would attempt to incorporate digital learning into their lessons for more engaging and interactive classroom instruction and were hard-pressed to do so successfully. The district had promised a 1:1 ratio of computers to students assuming that putting devices in their hands would equip them for learning from any place at any time. Yet less than eighteen percent of the district's student population had access to the internet at home. And, in reality, the district's students would need more than one device in order to access the internet from home and accomplish their learning goals and objectives.

The plan was for students to have a device that they loaned from their school campus for an academic year that had WiFi capability but did not come with a data plan. The district's 1:1 plan was unattainable because there was inadequate funding to support it.

So in my official capacity, I sought grant funding opportunities to equip the district with increased wireless connectivity so that there were hotspots set-up throughout the district that were in range for students to access from home. I also sought corporate partnerships and bidding opportunities to help cover and/or supplement the cost of cellular data for students needing to use their phones to connect all of their devices to the world wide web via their cell phone hotspot. Finally, I actively worked with school leaders to determine which devices required the greatest computing power (to include charging/electricity and connectivity) and which learning pathways those devices were best suited for. Clarifying and determining the need for charging stations throughout the district was generally unsuccessful due to a lack of support. Ergo, several students would share that they had the device that was loaned to them but that it was (more often than not) dead.

After just two months of being on the job and only three grant applications submitted, the school district was awarded a grant that was more than $1 Million. About thirty percent of that grant award was budgeted or earmarked for technology and bridging the district's Digital Divide. It wasn't enough to accomplish our *ideal* goals and objectives for bringing a world-class education to the district's students. But it was enough to ensure that we narrowed the accessibility and achievement gap with leveraged technology as best we could at the time. We sought more innovative ways to bridge the Divide with other grant and campus-specific fundraising and development pursuits.

Assembling grant project teams at the school district required many different approaches and types of expertise. Digital Inclusion involves so much and grant writing is not complete without digitally inclusive planning and implementation.

Digitally inclusive grant writing teams perform at their individual and collective bests in environments that are open source ecosystems. Self-reliance in a world that moves at such a fast pace is detrimental to growth on micro and macro scales. Building and belonging to open source ecosystems ensures that teams can produce value-added products, services, and results at a rapid pace, openly share information, and access data that will lead to exponential growth for the team and the organization as a whole. I once heard that the internet is the world's greatest library; the problem is that all of the books are scattered on the floor. The internet houses volumes of data that algorithms are turning into information that we use to make our lives and work a bit more lean and predictable. A good grant writing team understands the impressive potential volumes of data can have on the success and sustainability of their project and its outcome(s) and/or output(s). Also, good grant writing teams are cautious about how they access and share data so that it does not bring harm or ruin to the team, sponsoring organization, or supporting ecosystems. Good grant writing teams are composed of great storytellers.

Digitally inclusive grant writing teams are composed of a lead grant writing professional with the following characteristics (this list is not meant to be exhaustive):

☐ strong analytical and research abilities,

- strong writing skills,
- sensitivity to cyber attacks in their behavior and leadership,
- strong overall communication (verbal and non-verbal) skills,
- avid and (relatively) fast reading skills,
- strong organization and results-driven time management skills,
- adequate access to a vast array of computing devices with plenty of RAM and memory space (e.g., external hard drives with 1TB of storage capacity),
- unlimited access to Wi-Fi or cable broadband connection from home and work sites,
- strong knowledge of existing digital infrastructure and capabilities,
- good knowledge and understanding of digital archiving (to properly store data and to retrieve it to help predispose grant pursuits for success), and
- exceptional, consistently uninterrupted internet connectivity.

Digital inclusion is required for professional grant writing teams to be successful. As a fore listed, grant writing teams require a great deal of computing power and accessibility.

Professional grant writing teams are usually cross-functional and have the following general composition:

1. Planned beneficiaries,
2. Grant project champions,
3. Experts,
4. Innovators,
5. Visionaries, and in *some* more experienced/structured circumstances, benefactors.

Joshua Edmonds reminds us that "most people live in cities that are duopolies".[3] The Digital Divide is sustained, sophisticated and stratified, as well perpetuated by broadband duopolies throughout the nation, our states, our locales, and our world. Broadband duopolies have been a concern of consumer groups and the Federal Communications Commission (FCC) for over twenty years. And the number of internet service providers has not grown any more competitive than twenty years ago either.

For people looking to get connected, stay connected, or get better connected, broadband duopolies pose several challenges that include some of the following:

- Having limited, and sometimes restricted, access to broadband connectivity and high speeds, meaning that users cannot do what they need to do online and that their devices may lack the necessary connectivity for them to complete an activity or task online.

- Fixed service plans and costs, meaning that users cannot shop for products and services that suit their unique digital needs.

- A lack of digital infrastructure within range of their homes, meaning that users are limited to existing coverage within a short distance from their homes for optimal access to broadband and some mobile services. Most Americans use their phones to access the internet.

---

[3] Atkinson, Robert, Whisman, Jackie (2020) Podcast: Building Digitally Inclusive Communities, With Joshua Edmonds, https://itif.org/publications/2020/10/12/podcast-building-digitally-inclusive-communities-joshua-edmonds.

Actually, more Americans access the internet via a cell phone than a laptop, tablet, or similar device. This is especially true for lower-income Americans; this presents a unique problem that should be alleviated by more Public-Private-Partnership (PPP) initiatives throughout locales, states, and the national government.

☐ Having limited access to the internet of things, meaning that users cannot complete or perform critical activities and tasks because of their lack of access to devices that can be connected to each other.

☐ Inability for users to advocate for better products and services, meaning that users, in recent times, have lost the ability to connect personally and meaningfully with internet service providers to find and buy the best product, service, or solution for their internet service needs.

☐ Inability for users to protect themselves against data and privacy breaches, meaning that users are largely defenseless against cyber attacks and hacking. Generally, users are left unaware of how their information (e.g., full names, birthdates, geographic location, banking information, preferences, and other behavior while surfing the net) may be used without their expressed and knowledgeable consent.

☐ Unempowering communication and language used to sell to communities of color and women, meaning that internet service providers ordinarily target communities of color and women for education, outreach, and professional development using a very top-down approach to identifying, communicating, and implementing customer and talent recruitment. Rather than discovering how best to talk to and target communities of color and women through grassroots organizing, frequent (incentivized) focus group workshops and surveying campaigns, internet service providers, operating within duopolies, take for granted the diversity of its client base as there exists no other *real* competition.

The novel coronavirus pandemic has disrupted business as usual and has forced the world to contend with the tenable reality that recovery and survival, domestic *and* abroad, must be digitally inclusive. Access to the internet and access to devices that permit users to be entertained, work, learn, study, produce digital content, find and consume digital content, and other activities, is more important now than ever before.

The photo of thousands of cars lined up at the San Antonio Food Bank in April of the year 2020 speaks volumes of the indiscriminate impact that the coronavirus pandemic has had on people. Many Americans, especially the elderly or aging population, must decide between paying the rent or mortgage or making their car payment. For several years, the number of uninsured has steadily increased despite a markedly robust economy. I fear that the total number of individuals unable to access adequate healthcare due to work (or the lack thereof), having to take time to care for loved ones, and illness (especially illness related to aging, mental health and quarantine) during the coronavirus pandemic, has climbed well beyond the highest on record of 10% for the U.S.

I read that within just the last two years, some 90% of the world's data has been created. The latest statistic that I can gather is that 2.5 quintillion bytes of data are produced by humans every day. In an increasingly digital world, computing power is the greatest commodity that there is Maslow's Hierarchy of Needs has recently been modernized to include a smartphone with an unlimited data plan and fast and reliable internet access. Take a moment to picture the base of Maslow's triangular hierarchy listing the following of equal value and importance in one's life: air, clothing, food, shelter, sleep, and a smartphone with an unlimited data plan and fact and reliable internet access. The concept of digital parity has been introduced by authors Roberto Gallardo, Lionel Bo Beaulieu, Cheyanne Geideman (Oct 2020).[4] The paper is important for this book because it provides a compelling perspective supporting digital inclusion as a very fundamental and necessary element of grant writing and larger grant pursuits Overall, grant writing should be a principled process because its success has such great social impact and implications on its beneficiaries. Therefore, digital inclusion strategies that engage, educate, empower, and invest in communities affected by blight, divestment, and gentrification, are accountable, people-first or customer-centric, and ultimately sustainable. The Digital Divide will continue to widen if grant pursuits don't integrate digital inclusion strategies for the adaptation, benefit, and progression of all involved.

---

[4] Roberto Gallardo, Lionel Bo Beaulieu & Cheyanne Geideman (2020) Digital inclusion and parity: Implications for community development, Community Development, DOI: 10.1080/15575330.2020.1830815

Chapter 6

⚜

Fourth, Collaboration

Grant-writing is as strong as its collaboration. To ensure that a grant pursuit is worthwhile, grant project leadership should assemble members with different strengths and subject matter expertise to predispose the pursuit for success.

Collaboration on grant-writing teams involves planning *who*, *when*, and *where*. Collaboration is not a haphazard or unintentional exercise. Grant project leadership should have a very clear and explicit plan communicating the following critical aspects and expectations of professional grant-writing team members:

- *who* has the qualifications and capacity necessary to perform certain components of work on the WBS of the project, meaning that, for example, the grant accountant has the background and experience necessary to ensure that the grant project's budget is kept up-to-date with running planned and actuals columns and within compliance of internal and external requirements. *Who* also includes identifying strategic partners, providers, and other resources who may be invited to be on the team as part of your community of benefactors. Benefactors are powerful additions to professional grant-writing teams. They are usually very well-connected in the corporate and philanthropic communities and can help amplify the visibility of a grant project (new or existing). Benefactors are commonly asked to draft recommendation letters and pledge a match for a particular grant budget category or line-item to formally show their support for a particular grant project. Benefactors are also important to evidence the impact, growth potential, and sustainability of a grant project.

- ☐ ***when*** those team members will be involved and for how long, meaning that, due to budget constraints and/or other commitments, some team members may not have the ability to be involved in the grant project pursuit and/or awarded grant project on a full-time or part-time basis. Their time commitment may restrict them to a schedule of just four hours a day, three days per week. This is mission-critical for the grant project leader because limited availability may result in a delay in production for your project, delay progress on the duration of the project's schedule, and may even make the grant pursuit more burdensome than worthwhile.

- ☐ ***where*** those team members will be expected to work. Virtual and/or remotely located teams are not usually high-performing. In my experience, professional grant-writing teams get along with one another better, communicate past barriers, govern themselves and their team transparently, engage one another with care and trust, and deliver frequent value when they have had a good amount of time working together in person, rather than a virtual environment. Scheduling work around the team's availability to work in the same place is mission-critical. The coronavirus pandemic has disrupted our ability to work with our teams in the same physical location. I am a member of a few high-performing virtual teams. There are many unique aspects and features of the teams that make them different in comparison, but what each team has in common is their chemistry. There are no strangers on either team; we effortlessly and organically decide who will do what, when they'll deliver that work to the team, who will be responsible for management and oversight, who will properly account for and track our time, spending, and revenue generation, who will be responsible for telling our story and celebrating our wins along the way, who will sing our praises as a benefactor or participant spectator, etc. Working virtually requires us to communicate more often and to do so on different platforms that are easily accessible and agreeable to each team member. Though, my high-performing teams are also suffering from what is commonly called 'pandemic fatigue'. As the lead on the bulk of these teams, I govern frequent communication, so intentions are clearly conveyed with agendas that are time-bound and action-oriented.

Collaboration on grant-writing should always include a good look at existing public-private-partnerships. Several organizations interested in pursuing grants are usually looking for grant funds to sustain some aspect of their work or purpose over a long period of time. Scoring these opportunities provide organizations a great deal of comfort and opportunity to be more creative and deliberate in how they design their projects.

Chapter 7

✑

Fifth, Governance

Grant projects are not ordinary; they are vehicles of innovation and continuous improvement initiatives not usually governed by the line organization. Often, the environment that may have once fostered the innovation of a grant project changes and instead works against that innovation and jeopardizes a grant project's success. The reality of the impossibility of grant project success comes when plans do not have the likelihood of meeting actuals. Picture a simple x- and y-axis with a couple of running lines. One running line charts your grant project's actuals while the other running line charts your grant project's budget (i.e., this can be represented in dollars, time, or other KPIs) or plans.

My first quick tip: anytime that you read the word procure you should consider getting legal opinion(s) from a qualified source (e.g., an attorney or other sort of SME).

#1 Attrition

Staff are so important. To fulfill the requirements of a grant project and to ensure project success, staff roles must be defined, have shared responsibility on critical performance measures, and have clear organizational support with retention plans to prepare for the inevitability of change. Grant projects usually require a chain of command be in place to ensure that the administration and work of the grant upon award are not to be carried out by a lone staff member. The responsibility of fulfilling a grant contract is simply too much for one person to carry on their own. This is why most grant applications require multiple acknowledgments and/or signatures before they can be submitted. Most employers do not institute effective retention and succession planning at the onset of grant proposal writing and preparation. Succession planning is crucial as most contract awards require legally responsible contractual points of contact in fulfillment of the contract award. Succession planning ensures the retention of the contract award integrity and strategic purpose on part of the responsible department and larger organization when the realities of the impossibility of planned grant performance are realized.

#2 Unsatisfactory Performance

A grantor can request all or part of the funds it has given to a contractor for unsatisfactory performance. So, let's say, for example, that the contractor has been performing as planned. The contractor has been responsive and has been sharing progress at a monthly, quarterly and yearly frequency, but the quality of the work, from the contractor's perspective, is poor or wholly unperceived. Another example is from the internal or host perspective. The chain of command can also change in leadership or perspective and decide against continuing a particular grant project for reasons unbeknownst to the grant project team. When this happens, a grant project is starved to death. Be diligent about seeking legal expertise in these circumstances for a more formal presentation to the chain of command regarding the legal ramifications of withdrawing support for an awarded contract too soon. This commonly happens when leadership at the grant recipient's agency changes and strategic focuses and funding priorities change after the contract has already been awarded.

#3 Unforeseen Change in the Project Environment

Identifying possible or real risks to the success of a grant project is a practice that is required during the planning of a grant proposal and well in advance of contract award. But geopolitical events on a local, state, national and international scale take place unexpectedly and result often in direct or indirect impacts to our performance on contracts as contractors and even as buyers or grantors. Consider for a moment the churches operating food pantries before the novel coronavirus. For several months now, these service providers have either been forced to shut down their feeding operations or pivot to self-funding that operation themselves. Do you think that the number of people suffering from homelessness or food insecurity has decreased or disappeared since the pandemic? No, right. The need has increased and food insecurity is the worst that it's been in decades worldwide. Now let's consider an example of unforeseen change in the business environment from the perspective of the buyer or grantor. Consider a nonprofit grant-making entity who relied upon hotel occupancy taxes for monthly revenue. To make grants that they would issue as awarded contracts to other nonprofits in fulfillment of similar goals and missions to their own, they would debit a percentage of their monthly revenue to credit their endowment fund they issued grant funds from. The novel coronavirus has devastated the world and the hospitality and tourism industry was one of the first to experience its ruinous impact. A vast majority of projects have been halted, dramatically amended or outright shut down.

For many of our businesses (non-profit and otherwise), this pandemic has directly resulted in the impossibility of grant project success. Leadership during and through this pandemic will require us to actively seek and enlist the support of legal experts and other SMEs with hands-on experience and lessons learned ready to implement and scale for the success of more grant projects. This is how we will challenge the impossibility of grant project success so it ushers in a new normal for the performance of grant projects near and far.

Governance is a critical function of the leadership of an organization. Financial and program audits are commonplace in grant-writing and the overall grant management process. We have talked quite a bit about internal and external auditing in this book. The final words I will share on the topic are below.

Preparing for a grant audit, whether internal or external, can be quite intimidating. I can recall spending countless hours at work, sometimes even staying the night, creating new report templates, performing data quality checks, reading last minute updates to the Federal Register, finalizing budget narratives, and updating performance measures. Grant writing professionals are generally regarded as first-line technical assistance providers in preparing for audits, both internal and external, because of (a) their first-hand knowledge of the grant, i.e., its scope or performance of work, budget, management plan, deliverable schedule, etc. and (b) their stewardship of internal and external auditing controls, protocols, and